Copyright

Copyright © 1991 by Mission Creek Studios and Patti Jacquemain

All rights reserved. No portion of this book may be used or reproduced in any manner, stored in a retrieval system, or transmitted in any form or by any means, electronic or mechanical, including photocopying, recording or otherwise, without written permission from the publisher, with the exception of brief excepts used in connection with book reviews written specifically for inclusion in accredited publications. Requests should be directed to Mission Creek Studios, P.O. Box 23309, Santa Barbara, CA 93121

Neither this book, nor any part, nor any of the illustrations, photographs, or reproductions contained in it shall be sold or disposed of otherwise than as a complete book, and any unauthorized sale of such part, illustration, photograph or reproduction shall be deemed to be a breach of the publisher's copyright.

First U.S. Edition, 1991

Library of Congress Cataloging-in-Publication Data

Jacquemain, Patti, 1942 -
Sweet Seasons: Santa Barbara in Time and Color
    Includes Index
        1. Seasons of Santa Barbara
        2. Woodcut Prints
        3. Art
I. Title

91-62220 CIP

ISBN: 0-929702-01-8 (Hardcover)
           0-929702-02-6 (Paperback)
           0-929702-03-4 (Limited Edition)

Published in the United States by Mission Creek Studios, Santa Barbara, CA

Book designed by Anna Lafferty, Lafferty Design Plus, Santa Barbara, CA

Reproductions in this book are from photographs taken by Mission Creek Studios, Santa Barbara, CA

Printed in Hong Kong

In loving memory of my parents,
Christina and Arnold W. Jacquemain
and to the full and enriching days
we knew on Miradero Ranch.

*And to my good companion "Cajun" Cat
who while I worked sat and sat and sat . .*

Merry Christmas
Ron and Denny!
fondly,
Patti Jacquemain

11/23/91

ORWARD

Seasons rejuvenate the land. Their gift is the cycle of dormancy, rebirth, and growth. To one who loves the land - any land - seasons give us the variety that keeps our adoration aflame: the anticipation of surroundings that will change, along with the remembrances of conditions past.

Seasons also rejuvenate the human spirit. what inspiration a challenging winter, a colorful spring, the warmth of summer, and the blaze of autumn can bring! What enjoyment the travel, recreation, and learning accompanying the annual cycle can deliver!

Natural habitats are a source of my own inspiration. Appreciating them means immersion - hiking, sailing, photographing. Understanding them means being here, not one season but many, not one year but several. Cycles of drought, El Ninos, and wet episodes take decades to play out.

In this collection of original woodcut prints and writing, we see insights brought by Santa Barbara's seasons and settings to one of its natives. Patti Jacquemain is a talented artist who has unconsciously absorbed the moods and the color of the yearly cycle in her homeland over all of her life. Now, consciously, she translates her personal impressions of those moods and colors.

Taking in the message of this book will stimulate a sensitivity to the seasonal changes in Santa Barbara, a site often wrongly accused of having no seasons. This book has also afforded us the opportunity of having in one's hands a collection of Patti Jacquemain's prints. She has given us insight into what one who loves this special part of the world sees and feels as the earth tilts on its axis and brings transition to the land and our lives.

Dennis M. Power
Director, Santa Barbara
Museum of Natural History

Sweet Seasons
Santa Barbara in time and color
Patti Jacquemain

Preface
- FORWARD BY DENNIS POWER 5
- INTRODUCTION 9

Winter 10
- JANUARY 14
- FEBRUARY 20
- MARCH 28

Spring 34
- APRIL 38
- MAY 46
- JUNE 54

Summer 60
- JULY 64
- AUGUST 72
- SEPTEMBER 78

Autumn 82
- OCTOBER 84
- NOVEMBER 92
- DECEMBER 100

Final
- LIST OF ARTWORK 108
- THE ARTIST & HER ART 110

Pages from a journal

INTRODUCTION

Santa Barbara in Time and Color

Sweet Seasons? Yes, in Santa Barbara, a beautiful place where some say there are no seasons. Santa Barbara does have seasons. In the soft hues of the landscape, seasonal change is subtle. Summer's warmth turns hillside green to gold. Winter waves wash silver sand offshore to expose rocks below.

From the beaches, up the canyons to the high country, the wild country, our mild seasons change the fragrance and the feel of the air. Sounds change with the life cycles of animals and migration of different birds. Many are the signals of the seasons known to the perceptive, known to the Chumash, native people who lived in harmony with this fair land.

On soil rich with Chumash artifacts, my family had a lemon ranch in Santa Barbara. Weather was part of our life, be it dreaded frost or welcome rain. With a home nestled next to Mission Creek, nature was at my back door, a forest of live oak and sycamore. Roaming on horseback, I explored up the canyons, over the mountains, to the wilderness beyond. The seasons were sweet.

As a child I began to draw the world around me. Art became my life's work. Most of the images I create are woodcuts, an ancient art modernized by the use of many colors. With my art, verse, and writing, I weave a tale of sweet seasons. Guiding me are my journals which I have written and illustrated through the years. So now, in a way, I open a new journal of time and color.

As with the calendar itself, winter is a good time to begin a passage through Santa Barbara's sweet seasons. The first three months for most temperate regions is the dead of winter. Not so for our part of California. For us, the cold and wet of these first months signify rebirth.

Following months of drought, rain feeds life into withered plants. A succession of storm fronts march in from the Pacific Ocean. Laden with moisture, gray clouds give up some as they are lifted over the land. Brown and bare hills soon turn green with new grass.

Winter

A time of most turbulent weather, winter storms can stall and swirl overhead. Days of soaking rain swell creeks and rivers which rush seaward. Much of our landscape has been sculpted by such torrents through the ages, scattering sandstone through the land, water-washed stones and boulders of winters past.

Winter Beach, Carpinteria Beach in January

A new year! January is a beautiful time in Santa Barbara, a month with variety. It can bring sun-filled dry days when people cannot believe it is winter. Some years a bitter cold snap shocks us, doing damage to our citrus, avocado, and other tropical plants. It is a month of surprise.

Most exciting are the big winter rain storms, the kind January can bring. The downpour makes the creeks roar. These gully-washers have their own thunder, the deep rumble of large boulders rolling along in the creek's deep torrent. After the storm, when the flood subsides, it's interesting to see how the shape of the creek has changed, especially if it has scooped out a new swimming hole for summer.

Winter Break, Santa Cruz Island from Arroyo Burro Beach

Anacapa, Island from Camino Cielo

JANUARY DAYS ARE SHORT AND SWEET
IF THIS IS WINTER WHAT A TREAT!
A WINTER STORM MAY COME OUR WAY
BUT SELDOM DOES HARSH WEATHER STAY.

Storm Over Lake Cachuma, Golden Eagle at Lake Cachuma

Before the Storm, wind surfing at West Beach

Eventide II, Cypress over Butterfly Beach

Much of February's drama is found in the sky and on the shore. What a wet month it can be when swirls of gray rain clouds run before a Sou'easter, a storm feared by many yachtsmen. It is the time when the coast is exposed to the head-on fury of leaden swells with rolling caps of white. Without fail some poor boat is blown ashore to have its misfortune published as a newspaper photograph.

In the east, it's been said that "February depresses the soul." Here there is a subtle excitement as the earth comes alive again. In Santa Barbara, cool rains alternate with sunny days to produce a mantle of green. Leaves sprout from bare maples and sycamores. Lacy blossoms adorn fruit trees, violets bloom, and all over town pittosporum hedges fill out with new growth. For years people have come to winter in Santa Barbara. No wonder, for it is a vibrant time, a favored season.

East Beach

Clouds, cumulus rise over Santa Ynez Mountains

**Clouds may fill the February sky
shrouding the sun as they sail by.
The revived earth turns vibrant green
as precious rain brings a change of scene.**

Mission Dam, at Santa Barbara Botanic Garden

Colors of Winter

Squall, storm in the Channel

Lost Horizon, Sou'easter, East Beach

Fly a kite. It's March, coming in like a lion. The roar is up in the trees, the brisk breeze of a cold front clearing out. If rain follows, it's a brief shower from fat, fluffy clouds as they ride over the high mountains.

Seaward, the islands loom large on the sparkling horizon, their secret slopes shimmering in a rare light. Westerly wind prevails down the channel dressing the sea with flecks of running whitecaps. Soon they subside, calm returns, and the islands recede into their mysterious haze.

Was that a whale or a rolling whitecap? There are tales of tails of whales among the sails as people watch the channel. Many watch in this time of year when gray whales migrate north in anticipation of the arctic summer. If not whales, they may see dolphins ply the waters, the same as honored in Santa Barbara's Friendship Fountain.

Back in the hills, wild flowers appear, blossoms of many colors. Yet, color March yellow in its bloom of sour grass, goldfields, coreopsis, mustard, and acacia. With an eye for more than color, redtail hawks orbit over the slopes riding the warming air. They have a plaintive cry appropriate to the high station. Below, in the trees and deep in the canyons, smaller birds chatter in tune with the melody of the running creek. Windy or calm, the air is rich with sound.

Montecito, the Country Club from the bird refuge

Wind in the Palm, Channel Drive

When blustery winds bellow and blow,
The Blue-eyed Grass swings to and fro,
Dancing in the wind all day long,
Dancing to natures own sweet song.

Lupins, on the road to Solvang

Life seems fullest in the months rightly
known as spring. Indeed, bountiful
growth springs from a moist earth
warmed by successively longer days.
Plants flourish, as do the creatures
whose lives depend on them.
Young join the old and prosper
in a first season of life.

The air is robust, filled with the
fragrance of a thousand blossoms.
One can hear the joy of this good
season in full chorus, from soprano
hawks down to bass frogs,
a springtime song of life.

The days grow warm, and then
too warm, causing the earth to dry
and harden. The tempo of life slows
until coastal areas are wrapped
in dull, cooling fog, moderating the
heat of approaching summer.

Backcountry, Los Padres National Forest

Of the time we call April, the Chumash Indians said "month when flowers are in bloom." Bloom they do, nurtured by the mild rain of winter. Our mountains are covered with chaparral with blossoms so numerous that the cast of their green slopes lightens. The hills hum with the buzz of busy bees, and a natural fragrance drifts down canyons. Pollen is in the air and my nose knows it. For us, April breezes bring many sneezes.

Now with days longer than nights, we'll get a run of warm weather, a time when the earth seems to exude new growth. Often our first days of fog will follow, good days to weed and trim the garden. Above, the canopy of oaks is thick with new leaves. Below, there is a special freshness rising from the earth as late rain settles the source of hay fever.

Past and Present, Matilija Poppy and depiction of Chumash flowers

Quail

ENCHANTING SPRING IS IN THE AIR
　　FROM DISTANT MOUNTAINS TO THE SEA.
FRAGRANT FLOWERS BLOOM EVERYWHERE
　　HOW DELIGHTFUL APRIL CAN BE.

After the Rains, Santa Barbara Botanic Garden

Colors of Spring

It's bright so early on May mornings, and we make the most of the long daylight. More people seem to be out hiking in the hills, walking along beaches, lingering in the sun, and watching sails move across the channel waters.

Even at home, folks are out tending their gardens. Tomatoes are planted and strawberries are ready. As I spade my garden and turn the soil, robbins drop by to watch. I do the heavy work and they reap the worms and potato bugs.

Beyond the garden, out in the rolling hills the warmth of the long days takes its toll. The earth has given up much of its moisture, up the roots of thirsty plants. Without a clock, nature's schedule proceeds to finish the life cycle of grasses and other annuals. Green hills become mottled with ochre until life dulls under the coastal low clouds, the coming fog of summer.

Red in the Morning, channel, toward the sunrise

The sweet sounds of May can be heard
as songs arise from every bird.
The croaking frog and hum of bees
drift along on the soft spring breeze.

Pampas Grass

Wildflowers, on the way to Figueroa Mountain

In the back country away from the town,
How joyful to spend a few idle hours.
And to see this land often dry and brown,
Now covered with Spring grass and wildflowers

Fields of Fire

In olden days, the tale is told
Of a striking scene bright and bold,
   A sight that would inspire.

For mile after mile could be seen
Rising over a sea of green
   Radiant fields of fire.

This landscape that dazzled the eye
Of many travelers who passed by,
   Were poppies in the sun.

"California Poppy", their name.
"Cup of Gold", "Sleepy One", the same.
   Glorious every one.

Today freeways cover the land
Where fields of poppies used to stand.
   Now in gardens they grow.

Our state flower whom many love
Enjoy and think so highly of
   Still a colorful show.

California Poppy

Field of Fire

If there is one thing to be said about June, it is fog. Under the cover of darkness, its cool gray mantle covers coastal areas. Sometimes the persistent low clouds flood inland from the sea, up into interior valleys. At dawn a silent sea of gray is seen by those who venture high in the mountains.

Memories of school graduation, early summer vacations, and island trips are often colored gray by fog which shrouds the sun. That's early summer. Each day, from inland to the shore, the sun-warmed earth slowly burns off the fog. Yet, on many days the clearing never reaches the beach, to the dismay of shivering sunbathers.

Three weeks into the month is summer solstice. The sun reigns high over the longest day, and creative people form a merry parade which delights a new generation in Santa Barbara. What would the Chumash think of our celebration of the sun?

Mission Rose Garden

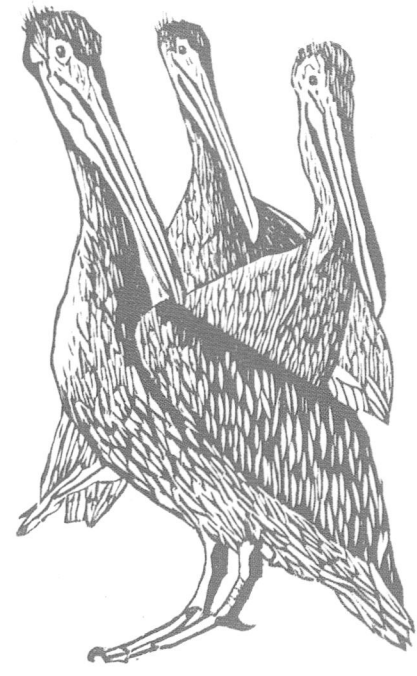

THE RAIN IS PAST, BUT SKIES ARE GRAY
FOGGY MORNINGS START THE JUNE DAY.
AFTERNOON SUN SHINES THROUGH THE MIST
ONCE MORE OUR CITY IS SUN-KISSED.

Southwind, island race in the fog

Dull days, cool days. Beyond the margin of coastal fog, green hills have turned to gold with the heat of each passing day. Rain is gone. Clouds are gone, and even the fog will retreat seaward as summer progresses. All creatures live below the clear sky. Blue above, and dryness below.

Up from the coolness of the seashore, relief from heat is found in the deep canyons wherever creek water still flows beneath the riparian forest. Out on the slopes, lizards scamper across heated rocks as hunting birds wheel about in thermals above.

SUMMER

An annual drought falls across a land caught in the clear between two great wind systems of earth. Summer showers and thunder are too far north following westerly weather fronts. Moist tropical trade winds are to the south.

With autumn at hand, and only then, is there the flirtation with the tropics, some weeks of humid warmth with fleecy cumulus overhead, clouds often painted by the setting sun. It is then, with a flash and rumbling, a thundershower may tease the parched land.

Oak tree, in Summer

Nasturtiums

From a hillside I watch the light of July break through retreating fog. It is a warm light from the high midday sun. Santa Barbara with its red tile roofs appears in soft pastel colors, shimmering without shadows. I look down to see my own shadow close by my feet, golden wild oats all about. The dry landscape glows.

In places where water is brought to the soil, in irrigated fields and home gardens, long sunlight works its magic with cultivated plants and trees. Plums, apricots and nectarines yield center stage to homegrown vegetables, the prize being red, juicy, sweet tomatoes. And our wonderful sweet corn, more than "knee high by the Fourth of July," is ready for a picnic in a backyard garden of agapanthus, hydrangeas, and bougainvillea.

Under oaks or by the sea, many townspeople gather for picnics in the friendly atmosphere of parks. Tables are set and children roam at play. As the blue sky fades to pink, the air of a July evening holds the delicious aroma of barbecue.

Backyard Bougainvillea

Summer Hills

Wild Oats

MELLOW DAYS OF JULY UNFOLD.
    DRY HILLS HAVE TURNED FROM GREEN TO GOLD.
JUICY RIPE FRUIT SO GOOD TO EAT.
    CORN, BEANS, TOMATOES CAN'T BE BEAT.

Journal pages - studies of:
Indian Corn, Cactus Apples,
Rhubarb, Tomatoes

Colors of Summer

Voices of children drift up from the creek. They may be from the neighborhood or visitors. August means vacation for many, a change of scene. Perhaps it's a change in seeing. On a downtown Santa Barbara sidewalk, I pass a tourist couple just as they see the courthouse for the first time. "Look at that!" one exclaims. At the corner, I pause to look at the building's familiar beauty.

In a world filled with noise, it's fun to escape to a quiet backcountry trail where one's footfall is surrounded by silence. There, sound is a quality of distance, a crow far up the canyon or a warm zephyr rustling the sycamore leaves just overhead. We rest in the shade, listen, and through the dry air hear a faint splash where creek water falls into a hidden pool. Soon it's our voices rising above the cool, refreshing water as we are in with the tadpoles, our toes in mysterious moss.

Crows

Moon Over the Mission, Mission Santa Barbara

Playing in the warmth of the sun
August brings us summertime fun.
As the full moon rises in the sky
"Viva la Fiesta" is the cry.

Backcountry Bear,
Black Bear as seen at Zaca Lake

Zaca Lake, the county's only natural lake

To me, more in mind than fact, September means the end of summer. School resumes, sounds of football are in the air, and then it seems that we get some of our warmest weather. How hard it is on captive students! Beaches are inviting, and the ocean is at its best for swimming. Funny how that works.

Deer come out of the dry hills in search of forage, even to browse in home gardens. In dry creek beds up toward the mountains, pools of water form as neighboring trees begin to shed thirsty leaves. Soon the night is filled with the happy croaking of frogs.

Change is upon us, and I am glad. I feel that September is a month to get through on our annual journey to the beauty of fall. Goodbye, September. Bring on autumn. It's a season of color.

Santa Cruz Island, north side

September Shadows, Sierra Madre Mountains

DUSTY, HAZY, PARCHED AND DRY,
SUMMER LINGERING, CLOUDLESS SKY,
HOPING, WATCHING, BUT IN VAIN
FOR SWEET, REFRESHING, EARLY RAIN.

Change is in the air.
Days shorten and
life's pace quickens.
Now the trees along
the creeks note time in color
as old leaves finish
their season of life.
Acorns drop to the delight of
chipmunks, squirrels,
and feisty woodpeckers.

 Autumn

Hot days return,
often with a wind called Santa Ana.
The fiery breath of the famous
general gusts into the night with the
frightening rush of dry leaves.
The fear is of wildfire.

Swiftly fire can consume old chaparral,
lofting ghostly plumes skyward.
Smoke masks the sun, and light
reaches earth as an eerie glow of death.
Creatures flee as best they can.
What perishes is born again,
for day by day the sun transits lower
until its solstice signal of rebirth.

Sycamore Leaves

In the news, we hear about autumn in the east long before we sense it here. Then there comes an October night as crisp as apples found growing in the Santa Ynez Valley. The harvest moon looms big and bright over our dry land.

Old timers hold that October brings the first meaningful precipitation. I always hope they're right. In the coolness of night the first rain often comes. It comes as a whisper, or is it the muted cheer of the land that we hear. The dust of summer is washed from every leaf, leaving the morning breeze to set the scarecrow dancing.

I see colors intensify. Pumpkins in fields glow in the sunlight, yellow leaves hang on willows, orange on persimmon, leaves that don't die for me. They say autumn.

The brightest red leaves are down by the creek. In their beauty they can be beastly. As my journal tells, "Drew poison oaks leaves today. Hope I don't get it!"

Autumn Glory, big leaf maple

Autumn Harvest, Goleta

Autumn Harvest II

October basks in autumn light
Golden grass has been bleached white.
Orange pumpkins and persimmons glow
Etching a colorful fall show.

Westwind, South Coast at Gaviota

Said a man from Maine . . .

YOU CALL
THIS FALL
WHAT GALL!

BONE DRY
CLEAR SKY
OH MY!

HOT DAYS
MUCH HAZE
FIRES BLAZE

I FROWN
THIS TOWN
IS BROWN

YOU SAY
FALL DAY
NO WAY!

Replied the local lady...

BUT WAIT
I STATE
FALL'S GREAT!

SUN SHINES
GRAPE VINES
GREAT WINES

I PRAISE
GOOD RAYS
BEACH DAYS

IS THERE
SOMEWHERE
SO FAIR?

I REST
THE WEST
IS BEST.

Some in life hang on. Others move on. That's my idea of November. While brown sycamore leaves ride out many storms falling in slow attrition until spring, not so the maples. Their big leaves glow yellow in cold sunlight for a short while. Then, in glory, they surrender to the earth.

There are lots of birds, including sojourners in migration. Many find their way to my feeder, while others join the robins feasting on red berries of the season. Some new birds are heard before seen, a new voice in the daily chorus. Then, when I least expect it, a visitor will pause on a nearby limb. We look at each other. I delight in the colored markings of a bird I don't know. Maybe the bird is not equally impressed, for in an instant he is gone, leaving me to rake leaves and plant bulbs for color in another season.

Autumn at Alisal, a view of the Santa Ynez Valley from the Alisal Ranch

Colors of Autumn

Great Horned Owl in the night

November nights descend brisk and clear,
    long nights proclaim autumn is here.
Grateful for this good land we share,
    Thanksgiving thoughts are in the air.

Deer in the Valley

Gazing at the tawny autumn grass.
How fast,
 How fast,
  The seasons pass.

Tawny Grass _____

Rice Grass II

December doesn't look or feel like the Christmas season we hear about. People who have come from other places know the difference. But to a Santa Barbaran, warm and sunny is the way Christmas feels, and it doesn't bear any resemblance to the wintry scenes seen on the greeting cards we receive.

Aside from the weather, there are subtle signs of the season in nature. The red toyon berries which I see in canyons and on hills say Christmas to me. And poinsettia! Their red and green leaves are the colors of the holiday season throughout the town, in gardens and as hundreds of potted plants.

There was a time years ago when December would find tall Douglas Fir trees growing in a line down the middle of State Street. Actually, those cut trees were placed and decorated by the city. About two to a block, right down the centerline, the trees were exciting attractions to be missed by motorists.

Saint Anthony's Seminary

DECEMBER DAYS SUNNY AND BRIGHT
WITH SPLENDID SUNSETS THAT DELIGHT.
COOL AND CRISP IS THE WINTER NIGHT
BUT CHRISTMAS DAY IS NEVER WHITE.

Poinsettias

ABOUT THE CHUMASH

They lived by the seasons. In their wisdom they worshiped the sun as the source of life's energy. They rejoiced in the falling rain when it restored the fullness of their land. To them, plenty and want were part of the sun's cycle, a reality of the seasons. Sustained by their environment, they could not have more than the yield of the seasons. They were the Chumash, native to this area.

As the sun made its annual transit from high in the summer sky to low in the winter, the Chumash watched the daily descent. Then would come the certain day when the shaman would tell all to stay in their shelters. The angry sun hung low in the cold midday sky. It was winter solstice.

Using a sun stick, a staff topped with a decorated stone, shaman skillfully pulled the sun higher. It never failed. In successive days and weeks, the sun slowly rose bringing new seasons of warmth and an end to the hungry time.

More variable was the rain. Water from the sky nourished plants, animals, and in turn, the Chumash. They did not grow their food, but relied on native vegetation. They hunted and collected all that they ate. From the ocean they could fish, from the shore they could glean shellfish, but it was only a supplement. The land was the true source of their food. A wet winter led to an abundant summer. Rainfall was vital.

By fall, acorns, pine nuts, and other seeds were gathered for the lean months to come. Stored food lasted longer if there was good hunting. In winter, migratory birds flocked to nearby wetlands. Some became food for the Chumash. If not, the long, cold nights were even more hungry.

People of the seasons, the Chumash waited for the turning, the moment when the sun would pass in and out of the condor's cave. With the benevolence of the sun, they would live well for another year.

104

AUTUMN

Winter Solstice, California Condor, Dick Smith Wilderness

WE DON'T FREEZE IN WINTER SNOW
NOR SWELTER IN SUMMER HEAT.

Winter Twilight

AS GENTLE MONTHS COME AND GO
EVERY SEASON IS SWEET.

List of Artwork

PAGE NO.	TITLE OF WORK	SIZE	MEDIA
End sheets	**Poppy Field** (portion)	14" x 9"	Woodcut
1	**Sweet Seasons**	42 x 29"	Linocut
4	**Poppy**	11 x 9"	Woodcut
6	**Matilija Poppy**	9 x 8"	Linocut
10/11	**Maple Tree**	18 x 24"	Linocut
12/13	**Winter Beach**	24 x 36"	Woodcut
14	**January Monarch**	6 x 4"	Linocut
15	**Winter Break**	13 x 8"	Woodcut
16	**Anacapa**	15 x 20"	Linocut
17	**Storm over Lake Cachuma**	24 x 18"	Woodcut
18	**Before the Storm**	18 x 26"	Woodcut
19	**Eventide II**	8 x 13"	Linocut
20	**February Scrubjay**	6 x 4"	Linocut
21	**East Beach**	20 x 14"	Woodcut
22	**Clouds**	13 x 18"	Linocut
23	**Mission Dam**	13 x 7"	Linocut
24/25	**Colors of Winter**	22 x 30"	Mixed Media
26	**Squall** (portion of print)	11 x 14"	Woodcut
27	**Lost Horizon**	9 x 14"	Woodcut
28	**March Daffodils**	6 x 4"	Linocut
29	**Montecito**	17 x 11"	Woodcut
31	**Wind in the Palm**	14 x 12"	Woodcut/Watercolor
32	**Blue-eyed Grass**	13 x 20"	Linocut
33	**Lupins**	13 x 8"	Linocut
35	**Peach Tree**	24 x 18"	Woodcut
36/37	**Backcountry**	26 x 37"	Woodcut
38	**April Quail**	6 x 4"	Linocut
39	**Past and Present**	27 x 20"	Woodcut
40	**Quail**	6 x 7"	Woodcut
41	**After the Rains**	24 x 18"	Woodcut
42	**Spring Bloom**	13 x 8"	Woodcut
44/45	**Colors of Spring**	22 x 30"	Mixed Media
46	**May Dolphin**	6 x 4"	Linocut
47	**Red in the Morning**	11 x 14"	Woodcut
49	**Pampas Grass**	19 x 15"	Linocut
50	**Wildflowers**	13 x 8"	Woodcut
52/53	**Field of Fire**	3 x 19"	Woodcut
53	**California Poppy**	7 x 6"	Linocut
54	**June Rose**	6 x 4"	Linocut
55	**Mission Rose Garden**	10 x 15"	Woodcut
56	**Pelicans**	10 x 6"	Woodcut

PAGE NO.	TITLE OF WORK	SIZE	MEDIA
57	*Southwind*	11 x 14"	Woodcut
59	*Solstice Sun*	6 x 6"	Linocut
61	*Oak Tree*	17 x 15"	Linocut
62/63	*Nasturtiums*	11 x 15"	Linocut
64	*July Thistles*	6 x 4"	Linocut
65	*Backyard Bougainvillea*	13 x 8"	Woodcut
66	*Summer Hills*	12 x 18"	Woodcut
67	*Wild Oats*	6 x 4"	Woodcut
68/69	*Journal pages, studies of Rhubarb, Cactus Apples Tomatoes, Indian Corn*	11 x 13"	Pencil/Watercolor
70/71	*Colors of Summer*	22 x 30"	Mixed Media
72	*August Sunflower*	6 x 4"	Linocut
72	*Dalliance*	9 x 10"	Linocut
73	*Crows*	13 x 10"	Woodcut
74	*Summer Sun*	9 x 10"	Linocut
75	*Moon over the Mission*	8 x 11"	Woodcut
76	*Backcountry Bear*	8 x 5"	Linocut
77	*Zaca Lake*	13 x 8"	Woodcut
78	*September Chipmunk*	6 x 4"	Linocut
79	*Santa Cruz Island*	13 x 8"	Woodcut
80/81	*September Shadows*	15 x 42"	Woodcut
83	*Sycamore Leaves*	15 x 21"	Nature print
84	*October Pumpkins*	6 x 4"	Linocut
85	*Autumn Glory*	11 x 5"	Linocut
86/87	*Autumn Harvest*	6 x 21"	Linocut
86	*Autumn Harvest II*	8 x 17"	Woodcut
88/89	*Westwind*	26 x 37"	Woodcut
91	*Autumn Sun*	15 x 21"	Linocut
92	*November Leaves*	6 x 4"	Linocut
93	*Autumn at Alisal*	13 x 8"	Woodcut
94/95	*Colors of Autumn*	22 x 30"	Mixed Media
96	*Deer in the Valley*	16 x 13"	Woodcut
97	*Great Horned Owl*	7 x 5"	Linocut
99	*Rice Grass II*	16 x 12"	Linocut
100	*December Toyon*	6 x 4"	Linocut
101	*St. Anthony's Seminary*	12 x 8"	Woodcut
103	*Poinsettias*	12 x 20"	Woodcut
105	*Winter Solstice*	27 x 20"	Woodcut
106/107	*Winter Twilight*	7 x 14'	Woodcut

The Artist and Her Art

    The best of all possible worlds for Patti Jacquemain is her niche in the cosmopolitan community of Santa Barbara, California. At work in the sylvan setting of her home and studio, she is an artist with both an international perspective and an appreciation of her immediate environment. When light and landscape are right, she often says, "That's a print!" Her mind's eye takes nature's form and color from the field, through days of studio labor, to produce on paper the best of her world.

    Drawing is the basis for Jacquemain's art. Her active mind and pencil have filled sketchbooks and journals since her childhood on a small ranch in Santa Barbara. Her favorite themes are the rural and wild, in part a response to seeing her ranch home disappear beneath the tide of urban development.

    Following high school, she was a scholarship student at the Choinard Art Institute in Los Angeles. She received her Bachelor of Arts degree in painting in 1964 from the University of California at Santa Barbara, where she would return for her Master of Fine Arts degree in 1974.

    In the years between university study, Jacquemain traveled through Europe and Asia exploring the settings which inspired great writers, poets, and artists. She worked in traditional media making her drawings come alive in mosaic tile and stained glass. Her interest in etching led to her MFA in printmaking, and in relief printmaking she found her best expression.

    For two years she lived afloat, sailing with the seasons between Florida and Maine. It was a life exposed to all weather and sea conditions, a time in which she created her collection "To Port and Starboard." She returned to life ashore with a sense of light on water still reflected in much of her art.

    Through the years Jacquemain's art has been exhibited nationwide in galleries and many regional museums. Her work is found in both private and corporate collections. UNICEF selected one of her woodcuts as a greeting card for international distribution in 1987.

STAGES OF WOODBLOCK PRINTING (Clockwise from top left). Journal with study, tools and carved woodblock, can and tubes of ink with brayer, mixed inks in glass, woodcut print with baren used to hand-rub image from woodblock to paper.

Jacquemain's printing plates of choice are wood. Using sharp steel tools she transforms her drawings and watercolor studies into carved woodblocks or linoleum, printing surfaces for oil-based inks. From cans of standard colors, she mixes inks to be the colors which she perceives in nature. Her mastery of blended color and rolled gradation on printing blocks produces her distinctive style.

Every Jacquemain woodcut is an original, matching others in the same limited edition. Drawing, carving, inking, printing, drying, numbering, and signing are all done by the artist. Her only studio helper is a half-ton press.

After she rolls on ink with a brayer, Jacquemain places the woodblock on the press. Over the inked surface she places printmaking paper. Registration is crucial, because the print makes many trips through the press. Each time, the unfinished print must be aligned precisely with the next carved block. When Jacquemain turns a large wheel, block and paper are compressed between heavy steel rollers. The impression is made.

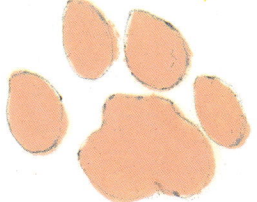

oh drat!
my cat
just sat

in ink
I think
she's pink!